WHAT OTHERS ARE SAYING ABOUT
CHRISTMAS WITH MATTHEW

"I remember the wonder of Christmas morning as a child with the family gathered around the Christmas tree reading the Christmas story before opening presents. Now you and your family can enjoy the wonder of Christmas every day in the month of December with *Christmas with Matthew*. Even the youngest family members will be able to feel and sense the amazing gift that Jesus is to our world. But more important than that, they will hear and see the power of Jesus to change each day from ordinary to extraordinary because he came on that first Christmas. With these daily bite-sized portions, the lives of "little ones" will be enriched."

–Carol Anne Friesen
Early childhood educator

"The Advent season focuses our attention each year on 'Jesus as Man.' In *Christmas with Matthew*, Pastor Scott Wade has masterfully presented a yeoman's work with this devotional using the gospel according to Matthew.

Whether one is just considering this Jesus for the first time or has been a lifelong follower of him, *Christmas with Matthew* will provide daily insight and helpful instruction in knowing and following Jesus as Savior. Thank you, Pastor Scott!"

–Greg Lyman, MD

christmas with matthew

Consider These Things

SCOTT WADE
with MATT & FAY WAGNER

dustjacket

ISBN: 978-1-953285-50-8

Published by Dust Jacket Press
Christmas with Matthew / Scott Wade with Matt and Fay Wagner

Dust Jacket Press
P.O. Box 721243
Oklahoma City, OK 73172
www.dustjacket.com

Dust Jacket logos are registered trademarks of Dust Jacket Press, Inc.

Cover & interior design: D. E. West / ZAQ Designs www.zaqdesigns.com
                    with Dust Jacket Creative Services

Printed in the United States of America

⬤ dustjacket

DEDICATION

This book is dedicated in memory of my mother, Velma Caldwell, whose childlike spirit still inspires me with the wonder of Christmas.

———— ✳ ————

CONTENTS

FOREWORD

When you are on a significant climb, you need not look back or down because what awaits you is ahead of and above! That is what we have come to experience and anticipate with Rev. Scott Wade guiding our spiritual climb higher and higher!

We are deeply honored that Scott would ask us to provide the readers of *Christmas with Matthew* with a pre-taste of the anticipation we feel regarding *Christmas with Matthew* both personally and with our church. While we may feel that our ministry credentials as founding co-pastors of a small Nazarene Hispanic congregation are overshadowed by Scott's extensive ministry accomplishments, we know he has been gratified by the impact his writing has had on us and our congregation.

You see, our anticipation for *Christmas with Matthew* comes from our experience with his previous devotional, *Christmas with Luke*. As in most Hispanic congregations in the United States, and I presume Canada, English is the primary language of our youth even though the adults may not be bilingual. Knowing that, we decided to provide both the English and Spanish versions of *Christmas with Luke* to each of our families. We also expanded their use from a daily devotional to a small-group study going over what we learned and what we spiritually gained during our weekly small-group sessions and our Sunday School lessons. The results were amazing. We witnessed spiritual growth and an increased hunger for God's Word as multiple generations accepted the climb!

We pray you will experience the same results as you make the *Christmas with Matthew* climb along with us and our guide, Scott Wade.

Blessings,
Bill and Isaelda Wojtkowski
Co-pastors,
Charleston (SC) Iglesia del Nazareno

ACKNOWLEDGMENTS

S pecial thanks to Matt and Fay Wagner—friends on the journey and fellow workers in the kingdom—for thought-provoking questions and activities geared toward children and families.

Thank you also to Lana, my wife, for her steady presence as I wrote this book and for her partnership in life and the gospel.

To Adam Toler and the staff at Dust Jacket—thanks for your wonderful leadership and expert advice in getting this project from plan to page.

I'm grateful for the work of my editor, Jonathan Wright, who worked hard so that the mess I made became an edition of excellence.

To the board at Momentum Ministries—thank you for joining me on this journey of ministry.

To all those who prayed, gave, and encouraged Momentum Ministries—thanks for making this and every other book possible.

To Bree Beamon, a friend and prayer warrior—thanks for your prayers and for contributing many of the written prayers included throughout *Christmas with Matthew*.

———— ✷ ————

INTRODUCTION

CONSIDER THESE THINGS

Now the birth of Jesus Christ took place in this way. When his mother Mary had been betrothed to Joseph, before they came together she was found to be with child from the Holy Spirit. And her husband Joseph, being a just man and unwilling to put her to shame, resolved to divorce her quietly. But **as he considered these things**, *behold, an angel of the Lord appeared to him in a dream, saying, "Joseph, son of David, do not fear to take Mary as your wife, for that which is conceived in her is from the Holy Spirit. She will bear a son, and you shall call his name Jesus, for he will save his people from their sins." All this took place to fulfill what the Lord had spoken by the prophet: "Behold, the virgin shall conceive and bear a son, and they shall call his name Immanuel" (which means, God with us). When Joseph woke from sleep, he did as the angel of the Lord commanded him: he took his wife, but knew her not until she had given birth to a son. And he called his name Jesus.* (Matthew 1:18–25)

Joseph, husband of Mary, was not ready to raise the Messiah in his home. As a matter of fact, he tried to get out of it. But as he considered these things, the Lord sent a messenger to tell him that this was exactly what he was chosen to do.

Matthew was an unlikely choice to be a disciple of Jesus, much less the author of one of the gospels. Consider these things: As a Roman tax collector, he was scorned by his fellow countrymen. He was especially unfit to write a Jesus story that was geared specifically for Jewish readers. But that is exactly what he was chosen to do.

When Matthew wrote about Jesus, the story was decades old. The religious authorities and the Jewish population alike had firmly rejected Jesus. Yet Matthew wrote in hopes that they would consider these things and accept Jesus as "the one who [was] to come" (Matthew 11:3).

There is no better time than Advent to for us to consider these things: how the coming of Jesus impacts us and our world.

Invite others to join you as you celebrate *Christmas with Matthew* and consider these things.

———— ✳ ————

ADVENT:
The Arrival of a Notable Thing or Person

A dvent is an anglicized form of the Latin *adventus*, which means "arrival," "appearance," or "coming." Christians celebrate the season of Advent in recognition of Jesus's arrival at Christmas. Traditionally the four weeks before Christmas are set aside to prepare for his arrival.

It is my hope that *Christmas with Matthew* will help you in your Advent preparations, to help you prepare for Christ's arrival.

While not following the Advent calendar strictly, this book will lead you on a journey to Christmas. Each day there is a suggested passage from successive chapters in the gospel of Matthew (or you can read the entire chapter!). There is also a unique devotional article, a prayer, and specific questions and reflections for that passage. Finally, there are activities and discussion guides for children and families each day.

I look forward to enjoying *Christmas with Matthew* with you!

━━━━━ ✳ ━━━━━

HOW TO USE
Christmas with Matthew

Since the dates of Advent change each year, this book is structured around twenty-four passages from the first twenty-four chapters of Matthew. These readings are presented for the first twenty-four days of December but can be adapted to the Advent calendar if desired. On Christmas Day the focus is Luke 2:1–20, the traditional Christmas passage. After Christmas you will find six bonus articles based on Matthew 25–28. These will guide you through the end of the year.

It is important to allow enough time for the Holy Spirit to speak as you work through the materials. It will probably take ten to twenty minutes to complete each day's journey. Of course, you can dedicate more time if you wish. Here is a suggested outline:

1. Read the passage (or entire chapter) of the day. This can be done earlier in the day and/or individually if that helps with your family dynamics.

2. Read the scripture focus mentioned before the devotional article. You may consider having everybody read this in unison.

3. Read the article. If there are two or more people, you may want to alternate paragraphs or take turns from day to day.

4. Recite the prayer that follows the article. If you are with others, have everyone read it together. If there are young children present, do a short paraphrase for the children to repeat.

5. Discuss the questions found in "Consider."

6. If desired, discuss and reflect upon the items in "For Further Study and Reflection."

7. If appropriate for your situation, complete the activities and discussion found in "For Kids and Families." If time is limited, you may want to choose this option instead of "Consider" or "For Further Study and Reflection." (Hint: Parents will want to look at these items beforehand to prepare.)

8. If you miss a day, don't panic! On the next day, stay with the schedule without trying to make it up. The articles are not dependent upon each other, and there is even some repetition of ideas for reinforcement. (You may want to designate a time to make up the ones you've missed, such as a Sunday evening or even on a day after Christmas.)

Are you ready for the journey to *Christmas with Matthew*? Let's get started!

———— ✳ ————

DECEMBER 1

Matthew 1 – Wake Up!

Read Matthew 1:18–25

When Joseph woke from sleep, he did as the angel of the Lord commanded him: he took his wife. (Matthew 1:24)

Are you so familiar with Christmas that you are "lulled to sleep" during Advent? It can get repetitious. Each year you hear the same stories, participate in the same activities, listen to the same music. If we don't consider the reason for the season, it can almost be like reading through the phone book.

Wait—that's how Matthew started his gospel! Much of Matthew 1 is taken up with the lineage of Christ. And while it may look like just a list of names, I would encourage you to give it your attention. There are some "undesirables" in the ancestry of Jesus, so we can be encouraged to believe that he accepts *us* as part of his family too! That was Joseph's good fortune, but he almost threw it away before he ever really understood it. Thankfully we read in verse 24, "When Joseph woke from sleep, he did as the angel of the Lord commanded him."

In his sleep Joseph had seen a vision. The angel of God had told him to go ahead and marry his fiancé, Mary. Yet Joseph couldn't follow through on that vision until he woke up.

Neither can we. In the Christmas season we experience the presence of God in a special way. We may even sense that God is speaking to us, but on December 26 we may find ourselves unchanged. It's because we are asleep. Advent is a time for us to wake up!

- Wake up to the presence of Jesus in your life and in our world!

- Wake up to the call to follow him in confident faith and bold action!

- Wake up to life-altering obedience!

May we all be stirred from Christmas drowsiness and respond as did Joseph—doing what the Lord commands!

Prayer: Lord, like Joseph, I am at times hard-headed and narrow-minded. At times I am asleep. Help me to wake up and do what you command me. Amen.

Consider: On the Internet or in other sources, research the different phases of sleep (N1—first sleep; N2—light sleep; N3—deep sleep; REM sleep). What happens in each phase?

Spiritually, what phase are you in? How can you wake up from where you are? Should you?

For Further Study and Reflection: Research sleep in the Bible and categorize the references into positive and negative.

Reflect: What are the benefits of sleep? What are the hazards? What happens if you get too much sleep? Too little? How do these questions apply to you spiritually?

For Kids and Families: Talk together about the funniest dream you have had in the past. Let everyone share his or her dream.

Talk about the importance of getting a good night's sleep. Remind the family that we don't want to go through the Christmas season "asleep." It's important that we remember why we're celebrating Christmas and to be wide "awake" when we're experiencing this season.

———— ✳ ————

✝

DECEMBER 2

Matthew 2 – Wise Men and Women

Read Matthew 2:1–12

*Behold, wise men from the east came to Jerusalem,
saying, "Where is he who has been born king of the Jews?
For we saw his star when it rose and have come to
worship him." (Matthew 2:1–2)*

Many of us grew up with Christmas programs featuring the wise men at the manger. It didn't matter that it wasn't exactly true to the biblical narrative. How many of you "played" (or wanted to!) a wise man? The Christmas story was not complete without them. Why? What's so special about wise men?

- Wise men *see*. Why did wise men from the East see the star while the religious scholars in Jerusalem missed it? Perhaps the scholars weren't looking for it. Perhaps they were preoccupied with their own interests. Or perhaps it wasn't where it was "supposed" to be. Do you ever miss the obvious things right in front of you? Wise men open their eyes to what is in front of them.

- Wise men *ask.* Perhaps the scholars saw it, but they thought they had all the answers. Wise men know that they do not have all the answers. Wise men are not too proud to ask for directions. They asked a great Christmas question: "How can I get to Jesus?" It's a question answered by opening the Bible.

- Wise men *come.* Their journey could have taken anywhere from a month to a year. Not knowing how long it would take, they still came; they still followed the star. No matter how far away from God we are, the important thing is to get turned around and start following Jesus. Wise men come.

- Wise men *worship.* They worshiped by rejoicing in the Child's presence, by falling down before him and by giving him gifts. Wise men worship in the presence of the Lord by humbling themselves before him. Wise men worship with great joy for sins forgiven. Wise men worship when they present their treasures—their very hearts—to God.

Are you a wise woman, a wise man?

Prayer: Lord, I thank you for the wisdom that only you can give and for your ongoing invitation to sit at your feet. As I pursue you, please give me wisdom to live out a life that is pleasing to you. Create in me an obedience and sensitivity to the Spirit so that I will put my faith into action daily. Amen.

Consider: Are you wise according to the above points? In what ways?

What does it mean to be wise in our own eyes? What does the Bible say about that?

For Further Study and Reflection: In his commentary on the book of Proverbs, Earl C. Wolf writes, "Wisdom . . . is mainly the application of the tenets of a revealed faith to the tasks of everyday living." Do you agree? How would you define wisdom?

Reflect: What does it mean to have a "revealed faith"? Do I base my life upon such a faith? How is that reflected in my "everyday living"? How is that not reflected in my life?

For Kids and Families: Play the "I Spy" game. For example, the first player may say, "I see something you don't see and the color of it is red." Take turns guessing until you figure out what the object is. Let everyone have a turn.

After the game, talk about not missing the real reason Jesus came.

As we go through the Christmas season, remind everyone to "look" closely to see what God is showing him or her.

———— ✳ ————

DECEMBER 3

Matthew 3 – Bear Fruit

Read Matthew 3:1–12

"Bear fruit in keeping with repentance." (Matthew 3:8)

On the inside I was thinking, *I don't like fruitcake.* But on the outside I was saying "Thank you so much for the Christmas fruitcake," because I loved the giver, my dear friend Wilma.

John the Baptist was the first excitement in years around those wilderness towns. The crowds were getting fired up. People were coming to God in droves—swindlers, prostitutes, oppressors, and even religious folk. Everybody wanted a piece of God. Or did they? John wanted to make sure that they understood what was at stake, that they were coming to God not on their own terms but on God's terms: "Bear fruit in keeping with repentance."

No matter how far we are away from God, what matters is that we get turned around to face God once again. That is repentance. But it must be more that believing or knowing the right things. That's what the religious folks who were coming to John wanted to do. They wanted to experience the excitement of the fire, the satisfaction of knowing that God was on their side. The problem was that they were not interested in making any true changes.

Jesus in his ministry continued along this line when he said, "If anyone would come after me, let him deny himself and take up his cross and follow me" (Matthew 16:24). Matthew—the writer of this gospel—knew what that was all about. He left his tax collector's booth in order to follow Jesus. He bore the fruit of repentance. And—miracle of miracles—he discovered that he loved this new life.

Do you want to know another miracle? A Christmas miracle? I discovered that Wilma's fruitcake was different from any I had ever tried before. I loved it!

If you haven't already, this Christmas try the fruit of repentance!

———— ✳ ————

Prayer: Lord, I am so thankful that you search and know my heart. Give me discernment to see the things in my life of which I need to repent. And, Lord, root me in a community that will hold me accountable to your Word. Protect my heart from the lies of guilt, shame, pride, greed, and condemnation that prevent me from running straight back to you. Amen.

Consider: What are the ingredients of fruitcake? What is unique or special about the fruit?

What is unique about the fruit of repentance? Why do so few people like it?

For Further Study and Reflection: Read 2 Corinthians 13:5; Galatians 5:15–26; and 1 John 1:5–2:6. Wait silently before the Lord as he speaks to you.

Reflect: What fruit of repentance needs to be expressed in your life right now?

For Kids and Families: Have an adult in the family cut up a piece of fruit and let everyone else try it with their eyes closed. Let everyone guess what kind of fruit it is. Talk about how the taste and texture were clues to the kind of fruit the person was eating. Let everyone share his or her favorite fruit.

What does today's scripture mean when it refers to the "fruit" of repentance? (Once we have turned from our sin, our lives "bear" good fruit—patience, kindness, goodness, self-control, and so on.)

———— ✳ ————

DECEMBER 4

Matthew 4 – From Darkness to Light

Read Matthew 4:12–17

*"The people dwelling in darkness have seen a great light,
and for those dwelling in the region and shadow of death,
on them a light has dawned." (Matthew 4:16)*

One summer my family vacationed for a week in the rolling mountains of central Tennessee. We stayed in a beautiful log cabin that overlooked an immense valley. There were no cities or villages nearby, the nearest homes were quite distant and unoccupied, and there were no streetlights. The first night there, we decided to turn off all the lights and go out on the deck. What we saw was beautiful! In that darkness the stars twinkled brightly and the Milky Way was easily visible. As a bonus, it was also at a time of a meteor shower. We saw scores of "shooting stars." We will always remember those dark nights on that deck.

Two thousand years ago the people of Israel were also in a dark, dark place. Subject to injustice at the hand of their Roman occupiers, the Jewish people needed the light of God to shine. Then Jesus arrived on the scene. A Light began to shine in the darkness. Some of the people flocked to the Light, glad for the hope and peace that he promised. Others, however, rejected the Light, choosing instead to remain in the darkness. They were afraid that the Light would expose their true nature. For those who followed the Light—when their deeds were exposed—they found forgiveness and mercy; they obtained everlasting life.

What darkness are you walking in today? What shadow is cast over you? Allow that darkness and shadow to be a blessing. Allow it to help you see the Mercy Way and the shooting stars of God's love. And when you see the Light, don't shirk away from it, but come into it fully and find forgiveness, mercy, and peace.

———— ✳ ————

Prayer: Lord, in this season of light, grant that those I love (including myself) would "open their eyes, so that they may turn from darkness to light and from the power of Satan to God, that they may receive forgiveness of sins" (Acts 26:18). Amen.

Consider: What exactly are "shooting stars"? If you do not know, research them. Why are we so excited by them?

For the purposes of bringing light to darkness, which is better—shooting stars, stars, the moon, or the sun?

For Further Study and Reflection: Read John 3:19; Matthew 6:22–23; and John 1:1–12.

Reflect: Where does God need to shine the Light of Christmas in your life?

For Kids and Families: Talk about different types of stars (such as stars in the sky, the Star of David, the star on your Christmas tree, sports stars, and so on). Give everyone a piece of paper and a pencil and see how many different kinds of stars you can draw.

Remind the children that when they see stars during the Christmas season, they should remember that God used a star to announce Jesus's birth and that he was a light shining in the darkness.

DECEMBER 5

Matthew 5 – The Perfect Baby!

Read Matthew 5:43–48

"You therefore must be perfect, as your heavenly Father is perfect." (Matthew 5:48)

She's perfect! I thought as I gazed upon my little Jenny. That same thought came back in two years with Emily and then in three more years with Amy. Were those newborn daughters really perfect? Could they walk with stability and talk with clarity? Could they conjugate verbs and subjugate emotions? Of course not! But that didn't limit the fact that they were perfect newborns.

Was the infant Jesus perfect? And how do you understand his perfection? As a baby, did he fuss? As a toddler, did he fall? As a teen, did he forget? As a man, was he frustrated? So was he perfect? Yes! At every stage of human development, Jesus was perfect.

In the "Sermon on the Mount" Jesus set a high bar for Christian living, but none higher than what he said in 5:48: "You therefore must be perfect, as your heavenly Father is perfect."

There is only one who can perform perfectly all the time, and that is God. Our performance can never come up to the highest standards of God's perfection. That's okay. The perfection Jesus taught was a heart that is perfectly set upon God.

So are we left without hope? No, for Jesus went on to explain how a true relationship with God changes us from the inside out. Perfection is that of heart transformation accomplished by the Holy Spirit in us. That's what Jesus is looking for. He knows that if our hearts are right, then right actions will soon follow.

Do you long to please God? Do you want to live up to the high standards of love, holiness, and purity? Do you want to serve God with all your might? Then get your heart right. For when the heart is right, everything else will follow.

Prayer: Lord, help me to surrender and yield to your Spirit. It is only by the blood of Christ that I am transformed and made new. Help me to see your perfection despite my circumstances, and create in me a heart that yearns to reflect you in both thought and action. Protect me from putting my identity and worth in my performance, and allow me to see myself the way you do. Amen.

Consider: Can a rainy day be perfect? How?

In what ways are babies perfect? Imperfect? What about teens? Adults? Biblical perfection has to do with coming to completion or to fulfilling an intended purpose. How does that alter your answers to the above?

For Further Study and Reflection: Reflect upon Ezekiel 36:26–27 and Acts 15:8–9. These verses relate heart cleansing with the giving of the Holy Spirit.

Reflect: Do you believe that God is able to perfect your heart? Have you asked him to do that very thing for you through the indwelling of the Holy Spirit?

For Kids and Families: Wad up some pieces of paper and take turns throwing them at a trash can. Allow everyone to try to get a perfect score of ten baskets in a row. What happened when they tried to get a perfect score? Was anyone able to do it?

Remind the children that while we can never live without making some mistakes, it is possible to allow God to make our hearts perfect.

Have a time of prayer together asking God to make each one's heart perfect.

✝

DECEMBER 6

Matthew 6 – Mixed Feelings

Read Matthew 6:25–34

"Therefore I tell you, do not be anxious about your life, what you will eat or what you will drink, nor about your body, what you will put on. Is not life more than food, and the body more than clothing?" (Matthew 6:25)

We were in the airport and I had mixed feelings. I've always admired those willing to share God's love overseas, and I was very excited about our mission trip. But I was not a fan of international travel. My quiet five acres in Bethel, Ohio, suited me just fine! We do not always do what we're comfortable doing. So at times we need to hear those words: "Do not be anxious."

As I departed on that mission trip to Costa Rica, God reminded me that I didn't need to be anxious—not even about preaching through a translator, something I had never done before! God reminded me that he had given us great team leaders in Matt and Fay. He reminded me that he had placed missionaries in Costa Rica who would help us with our mission.

I wonder how Jesus felt when he made his mission trip on that first Christmas. Did he have mixed feelings? Did he need to hear, "Do not be anxious"?

When Jesus told his listeners, "Do not be anxious about your life," he didn't say, "Do not be concerned," or "Do not take the necessary steps," or "Do not work." Just as our mission trip required careful planning and work to make it happen, so our lives deserve careful attention. Not being anxious is very different from not being responsible! In verse 26 Jesus indicated that the birds of the air are not toiling too hard, but God feeds them. Jesus was saying in effect, "If God feeds the birds, who do not sow or reap, won't he even feed *you* more—you who *do* sow and reap?"

So do your part and don't worry about it. God is in control!

———— ✳ ————

Prayer: Lord, help me to remember that gaining you is worth giving up all my control and comfort. You are bigger than my fears. Allow me to embrace your goodness, compassion, peace, and instruction. I choose to take my thoughts captive and meditate on your truth despite my circumstances. Amen.

Consider: In what unexpected ways did God show that he was in control of Jesus's life on that first Christmas? In what ways is he showing you that he is in control of your life this Christmas?

If you are anxious about your life, what should you do?

For Further Study and Reflection: How does Galatians 4:4 help relieve your anxiety? What about 1 Peter 5:6–7? What other verses have helped you in times of anxiety?

Reflect: Think about some of your most anxious times. How did God give you peace? Reflect upon Isaiah 26:3: "You keep him in perfect peace whose mind is stayed on you, because he trusts in you."

For Kids and Families: Allow each member of the family to tell about a time when he or she felt anxious (such as the first day at a new school, moving to a new town). Then listen to "Silent Night" together or read the lyrics.

How does the advent of Jesus bring peace to the world and to our hearts?

Discuss how the hope of Jesus with us brings peace and calm.

———— ✳ ————

DECEMBER 7

Matthew 7 – Christmas Present

Read Matthew 7:7–12

"You will recognize them by their fruits." (Matthew 7:20)

"You can't judge me. You don't know my heart." Have you ever heard that?

It's not entirely true. We can know a good deal about people by observing their actions. Or, as Jesus said, "You will recognize them by their fruits."

- Many people can make their *case*. They can say the right words, but words are probably the least reliable indicator of their hearts.

- Others can put the right *face* on things. They can mask who they really are with an aura of spirituality. Jesus had a name for people who wore masks—*hypocrites*!

- Some feel that they are the right *race*. They feel that they have special privileges and deserve special treatment because they have a special status. Jesus was never impressed with people's pedigrees!

- Others insist on their *place*. They elevate their own importance. Jesus advised us to "take the lowest place."

- Some want to be judged by their intentions, by what they *chase*. As a child I often told my mother, "I'm going to . . ." She often reminded me that the road to loss is paved with good intentions. We need to be doers of the Word!

Not only can we know others by their fruit, but we can also know *ourselves* by *our* fruit. Paul said, "Examine yourselves, to see whether you are in the faith. Test yourselves. Or do you not realize this about yourselves, that Jesus Christ is in you? — unless indeed you fail to meet the test!" (2 Corinthians 13:5). This is more than introspection. He was urging us to be objective—to see what kind of fruit our faith is producing.

At Christmas it is especially easy to satisfy ourselves with substitutions for vital faith. But ask yourself, "Does my fruit pass inspection?"

———— ✳ ————

Prayer: Lord, Lord . . . I don't want to just *talk* about the kingdom of God. I want to be in—*fully in*—the kingdom. Help me to produce the fruit of the kingdom. Amen.

Consider: I once heard someone say, "I may not be a judge, but I *am* a fruit inspector." What is your response to that statement? What negatives outcomes might be associated with it? Positive outcomes?

When it comes to inspecting fruit, do you tend to be harder on others or on yourself?

For Further Study and Reflection: In Galatians 5 Paul writes about the *works* of the flesh and the *fruit* of the Spirit. What if anything is significant about his choice of words?

Reflect: How can I eliminate the works of the flesh? How can the fruit of the Spirit be increased in my life? How are these things related?

For Kids and Families: Choose one member of the family to be "it" and have that person close his or her eyes. The others decide on one person to say, "Merry Christmas," in a disguised voice. See if the person with his or her eyes closed can guess who said it. Play more rounds until everyone gets a turn to participate. Talk about what clues gave away the identity of the speakers.

Just as our voices can't be totally disguised, our hearts will reveal who we really are.

It's important to examine ourselves to make sure we're producing good fruit.

———— ✳ ————

DECEMBER 8

Matthew 8 – What Kind of Person Are You?

Read Matthew 8:23–27

The men marveled, saying,
"What sort of man is this?" (Matthew 8:27)

After Jesus's birth, Joseph and Mary presented him at the temple according to the law. There they *marveled* when Simeon called Jesus "a light for revelation to the Gentiles, and for glory to your people Israel" (Luke 2:32).

That wasn't the last time Jesus caused people to marvel. When Jesus calmed the storm, saving the lives of his disciples, they asked, "What sort of man is this?" They marveled at him. I believe that they had a little fear and amazement mixed in together—a little of both the negative and the positive.

"What kind of person are you?" That question can be asked from two perspectives. One perspective is negative: "How could you do this *to* me? Just what kind of person are you?" The other perspective is positive: "Why would you do this *for* me? What kind of person are you?"

Which perspective do you want to leave? Do you want to leave people muttering to themselves, "How could she do that to me?" Cross words, careless actions, and caustic attitudes leave behind an atmosphere of anger, mistrust, and pain. The world will be a little darker, a little less hopeful, if we are mean-spirited or high-minded. Wouldn't you rather leave people marveling to themselves, "Why would he [she] do that for me?" A kind word, a helpful deed, and a forgiving spirit will leave behind the aroma of Christ. The world will be a little brighter, a little more joyful, a little easier to take.

What kind of person are you? Today we will cause people to ask that question—perhaps not consciously, but they will ask. And our lives will answer! During this season, let us resolve to leave people with the positive perspective!

❋

Prayer: Lord, go with me today. Be in me that divine Light that will make people marvel and not mutter. I want to spread your kingdom and your kindness everywhere I go today. Amen.

Consider: Think back over your day yesterday. Did anyone cause you to think, *How could he [she] do that to me?* What can you do about it? Did anyone cause you to think, *Why would he [she] be so kind to me?* What should you do about that?

How about your actions? Did you leave behind hurt feelings? What should you do about it?

For Further Study and Reflection: In Matthew 8:26, *before* Jesus calmed the storm, he asked and answered a question. What was the question? What was the answer? In Matthew 8:27, *after* Jesus calmed the storm, the disciples asked and answered a question. What was the question? The answer?

Reflect: What is the significance of *before* and *after* above? What storms are in the *before* stage in your life? The *after* stage? How can the answers above help you?

For Kids and Families: Think together about a way your family can do a kind deed to cause someone to ask, "Why would he [she] do this for me?" Then decide as a family how and when you will do it. Perhaps you could make a phone call to someone who needs encouragement, or make handmade Christmas cards for a shut-in.

What kind of family are we? How do we want people to remember us?

———— ✳ ————

DECEMBER 9

Matthew 9 – Risky Prayer

Read Matthew 9:35–38

*Then he said to his disciples, "The harvest is plentiful,
but the laborers are few; therefore pray earnestly to
the Lord of the harvest to send out laborers into
his harvest." (Matthew 9:37–38)*

That is a risky prayer to be prayed! Jesus is moved when he sees crowds of people who are without hope, and if we pray earnestly for him to send out laborers, he just might send *us*! Notice some things from this passage:

Jesus was proactive and pro-people!

- He went around doing the work of the kingdom. He wasn't content to say, "Let them come to me." So often we adopt the attitude that people can find their way to Christ.

- He saw people who were harassed. "Harassment" today may come in the form of social media doxxing, threat of terror, economic fear, uncertain health care, and crumbling morality.

- He saw people who were helpless. The people of his day could do nothing against oppressive Rome. People today feel helpless against the forces of government bureaucracy.

- He saw people who lacked guidance and care—without a shepherd. In the midst of their harassed and helpless condition, they had no one to show them a better way, no one to join them in their suffering.

Jesus's heart was moved. So he challenged his disciples—To see the same things he saw. Do we have eyes for the harvest?

- To pray for God to send "shepherds" to those people. Are we struck by the lack of caring, guiding voices among people who are away from God?

- To be willing to go as workers into the harvest field. This challenge was implicit rather than explicit. But all we know from the teachings and mission of Jesus is a challenge to us to be willing to go and bring help

Christmas reminds us that Jesus was proactive and pro-people. Let the Spirit of God challenge you to be the same.

———— ✳ ————

Prayer: Thank you, Lord, that your heart is moved with compassion for the harassed and the helpless—including me! Send out workers to share the good news of your love. Help me to have a heart like yours, that I may be willing to go. Amen.

Consider: In what ways is the harvest plentiful today? Is there an abundance of laborers?

What actions at Christmas would indicate that you are proactive and pro-people?

In what ways is Christmas a good time for laboring in the harvest?

For Further Study and Reflection: What takes place immediately after Jesus instructed his disciples to pray that risky laborer-sending prayer in Matthew 9?

Reflect: Have you prayed that risky prayer for the Lord of the harvest to send out laborers? What is his answer to you? What is your answer to him?

For Kids and Families: Talk as a family about what it actually looks like to be a laborer in the harvest. Come up with ideas to live out being laborers in the harvest. Make a list of your ideas as a family and commit to carrying out one of your ideas during the Christmas season.

———— ✳ ————

DECEMBER 10

Matthew 10 - Full House

Read Matthew 10:3–16

"Behold, I am sending you out." (Matthew 10:16)

Many years ago a popular song by the Lanny Wolfe Trio included lyrics in which Jesus said that his house is full but his fields are empty, that his workers all want to stay around the table rather than going into the field to harvest the grain. That song is needed more today than it was then.

God has always had work for his children. Adam was placed in a garden of life and beauty, but God also called him to tend to his creation. Noah and his family were saved from the flood waters, but God gave Noah the assignment of building the ark. Abraham was to be the father of nations, but God also assigned him to bless the nations.

The Bible is a story of God partnering with people to accomplish his purposes. He partnered with Adam, with Noah, and with Abraham. He also partnered with Mary and with Joseph to bear and raise Jesus. So when Jesus sent out his disciples in Matthew 10, he was simply continuing this God pattern.

Do you think that God's methods have changed? Does he not still call people and send them out to do the work of the kingdom? Should you be surprised that God's call and sending include you? Are we to think that serving God is only about going to church on Sunday and getting our spiritual appetites fed and our spiritual fancies tickled?

Before he sent the disciples out, verse 1 says that Jesus called them to him. At Christmas remember that God calls us to him for worship, for inspiration, for encouragement—but also for instruction. We receive our "marching orders" and are to go out on mission. Where is God sending you?

———— ✳ ————

Prayer: O God, as you send me out, remind me that "when the fullness of time had come, God sent forth his Son, born of woman, born under the law, to redeem those who were under the law, so that we might receive adoption as sons" (Galatians 4:4–5). And help me to obey. Amen.

Consider: Do you personally know any missionaries? Who are they and where do they serve? Pray for them and their work.

How are these missionaries different from you? How are they the same as you? Based on that, how should you pray for yourself right now?

For Further Study and Reflection: Who is William Carey? Why is he called "the father of modern missions"?

Reflect: Who would you say is "the father of biblical missions"? Consider what can be learned from the lives of these missionaries: Jonah (Jonah 1–4); Philip (Acts 8); Peter (Acts 11); Barnabas, John Mark, and Paul (Acts 13–20).

For Kids and Families: Let everyone share what he or she thinks the word *missionary* means. After everyone has shared, look up the definition of the word. Does that definition match your understanding of what it means to be a missionary?

How can you be a missionary in your own community? Discuss ways God can use each of you as missionaries, and close with a time of prayer asking him to do so.

✝

DECEMBER 11

Matthew 11 – Do You Get It?

Read Matthew 11:25–30
*"I thank you, Father, Lord of heaven and earth,
that you have hidden these things from the wise and
understanding and revealed them to little children. . . .
No one knows the Father except the Son and anyone to
whom the Son chooses to reveal him."* (Matthew 11:25, 27)

My friend bragged, "I got a PhD!"

"You did?" I asked skeptically.

"Yep!" he said. "I got a post hole digger!"

Have you gotten a PhD? Don't worry—

- You don't have to have a PhD to "get it." The way of salvation is not hard to understand. The Old Testament prophet said, "Even if they are fools, they shall not go astray" (Isaiah 35:8). All we need to do is hold on to the hand of the One who leads us.

- God wills that we "get it." God has not made it difficult to find him. The apostle Paul said in his sermon at Lystra that God "did not leave himself without witness, for he did good by giving you rains from heaven and fruitful seasons, satisfying your hearts with food and gladness" (Acts 14:17). God desires that all come to the knowledge of salvation.

- Finally, without Jesus, we will never "get it." In another place Jesus said, "I am the way, and the truth, and the life. No one comes to the Father except through me" (John 14:6). We may try all sorts of other routes, but only one way leads to God: Jesus Christ. All other ways are at best detours and at worst dead ends.

Calleigh and Colton, our youth pastor's children, walked with me into the parking lot after church. Five-year-old Calleigh instinctively grabbed my hand. I then reached out to three-year-old Colton, who quickly did the same. The way was in reach. Even children can "get it." Do you?

People often say that "Christmas is all about the kids." While I might argue differently, Jesus said something quite like that when he said that God had revealed the kingdom to little children and that little children enter the kingdom. They get it.

———— ✳ ————

Prayer: Thank you, Lord, for revealing the way of the kingdom to me. I deny myself and take up my cross today to follow you. Amen.

Consider: Did you come to Christ as a child, as a youth, or as an adult? How was Christ "revealed" to you?

What did you understand about Christianity when you first believed? Has your understanding changed? If so, in what ways?

For Further Study and Reflection: Think of the biblical symbols around Christmas. What do they convey about the character of Christ?

Reflect: How is Christ revealed (portrayed) in our modern celebrations of Christmas? How is it helpful? Harmful?

For Kids and Families: See how fast each member of the family can say the letters of the alphabet. Don't be afraid to get silly with this! Take this opportunity to present the ABCs of salvation to your children:

- A = We are all sinners and must ADMIT this.
- B = We must BELIEVE that Jesus died to save us from our sins.
- C = We must CONFESS that Jesus is Lord and offer our lives to Him.

Take time together to pray. Allow your children the chance to pray a prayer of salvation if they have not already done so. Even children who have prayed for this before may find comfort in offering themselves to Jesus again.

———— ✳ ————

DECEMBER 12

Matthew 12 – "Chreasters"

Read Matthew 12:9–14

And it was restored, healthy like the other. (Matthew 12:13)

Do you know what "Chreasters" are? You know—those who come to church only on Christmas and Easter. Sometimes they are called "Santas and bunnies." What's their problem? Maybe "their" problem is really "our" problem. Maybe church folks aren't reflecting the love and life of Christ as they should throughout the year. Maybe when Chreasters come they feel just a bit of judgment.

In Matthew 12 Jesus met a man "with a withered hand" in the synagogue. (Not everybody in church is in mint condition!) Wisely, the man had refused to let his withered hand keep him away from the place of worship. He was determined to come to church no matter what others thought, said, or did. He was not a Chreaster!

What causes Chreasters in the church?

- Some people let their own faults keep them away from church and God. They reason, "When I get my life straightened up, then I'll come to God." That is a lie from Satan! No person can get his or her life straight enough to come to God.

- Other people let the faults of others keep them away from church: "Why should I go to church? They're no better than me." That is the truth from Satan! It is often true that the people in the church are no "better" than those away from God. But if we used that same logic, we would not go to the doctor or hospital, because the people there are just as sick—or sicker!—than we are.

This season determine that you are going to exhibit the love and life of Christ all through the year. And if you see a Chreaster, pour out an extra measure of grace. After all, you need it just as much as all the Santas and bunnies!

———— ✳ ————

Prayer: Lord, I repent of the times I have misrepresented the body of Christ and have pursued personal comfort over the growth of your kingdom. Help me to be a healthy and active part of the body of Christ. Give me the wisdom to build intentional relationships and stand in unity with my brothers and sister in Christ. Amen.

Consider: Think about the withered hand of the man in the synagogue. Describe it. What did it look like? What could it do? What could it not do, and by extension, how were the man's life and family hampered?

Now think about your own spiritual hands. Are they withered? In what way? What do your spiritual hands look like? What can they do? What can't they do? How are they impacting your life, family, and church?

For Further Study and Reflection: Do a quick review of the gospels and note every time Jesus sees sickness—either physical or spiritual. Based on his response, what is his attitude toward sickness?

Reflect: Are you, or is someone you know, sick either spiritually or physically? What is Jesus's attitude toward you or them?

For Kids and Families: Challenge everyone in the family to a small task, but add the stipulation that only one hand can be used to accomplish it. For example, try to fasten a button, zip a coat, peel a banana, or make a peanut butter sandwich with one hand.

How does using only one hand hamper the ability to complete a task? Remind everyone that we shouldn't allow our shortcomings (or the shortcomings of others) to keep us from God or the church.

※

DECEMBER 13

Matthew 13 – A Good Story

Read Matthew 13:10–17

"This is why I speak to them in parables." (Matthew 13:13)

I love my grandchildren to come home for Christmas! We do many things together, but one of their favorites is for *Pahpooh* (that's what they call me!) to tell them "The Monkey Story." It's a really good story, but they've heard it so many times they now know it by heart. They begin losing interest or start telling their own versions. Sometimes they get it right, and sometimes they don't.

The story of Christmas is like that. We've heard it so many times that we can lose interest, or we retell it with our own meanings attached.

Every Christ-follower has a story to tell, and people "read" those stories every day. The apostle Peter—himself an eyewitness to the story of Jesus—said, "In your hearts honor Christ the Lord as holy, always being prepared to make a defense to anyone who asks you for a reason for the hope that is in you; yet do it with gentleness and respect" (1 Peter 3:15).

Everybody loves a good story—to hear and to tell. Jesus recognized this, so he told people many things in parables. A story communicates a message much more powerfully than a recitation of facts and formulas. People identify with and remember stories that touch their hearts.

This Christmas live the story of how Jesus touched your heart. People will read it and remember. Make Christmas fresh and meaningful by adding something new to your Christmas traditions. Also, make sure that Jesus doesn't get crowded out of your family celebrations.

———— ✳ ————

Prayer: Lord, my story may not seem exciting to others, but I thank you for allowing me to live it. Help me to share the story of your love with others. Help me to do that with gentleness and respect. Amen.

Consider: What was your favorite story as a child? Who told it to you? What drew your heart to that story—the teller? Suspense? Courage? Excitement? Humor? Love? Surprise?

Has God ever spoken to you in a story? What was it about? What did you do?

For Further Study and Reflection: Look up the parables of Jesus (You can find them online at *https://www.gotquestions.org/parables-in-the-Bible.html* or in other sources). Which of them are the most meaningful to you? Why?

Reflect: Imagine writing a parable of Christmas. What is the message you want to convey? Who are the main characters? What is the setting? What actions take place? Now write it down and share it with someone.

For Kids and Families: Play a "story game." Each person gets a turn saying a word or phrase, and then the next person adds another word or phrase. Continue until everyone has had a turn or you feel that the story has come to a conclusion. Remind the children that God often speaks to us in stories.

After the game is over, tell your own story of how you came to know Christ. Allow other family members to share if desired.

DECEMBER 14

Matthew 14 – Alone

Read Matthew 14:22–33

When evening came, he was there alone. (Matthew 14:23)

Christmas is a noisy time, isn't it? When my family gets together, nineteen of us are under the same roof. Games, laughter, television, music, and crying babies come together in an overwhelming cacophony. Sometimes I just need to retreat to a quiet place to be alone.

Do you ever get worn out by people? Are there times when you need to be alone? Jesus had those times. Crowds could wear him out. Even his closest friends could tax him to the limit. Then he would go off by himself. In Matthew 14 he experienced such a time and went up on a mountain to be alone—with God.

Time alone with God will help you during the Christmas season and all year long. But you need to be intentional as was Jesus:

- Jesus sent the disciples away, saying in essence, "I want to be with you, but not now. I have something else that I just have to take care of." Are you able to send people away so you can be with God?

- Jesus dismissed the crowds who demanded his constant attention. They were important to Jesus, just as were his friends, and they were the reason he had come. But even the crowds had to take a back seat at times while Jesus was alone with his Father. There are times in all our lives when even legitimate demands must give way.

- Finally, Jesus went up the mountain, where he would not be disturbed. He needed quiet, undistracted time when he could not only talk to but also hear from God. In modern parlance, it was no TV, no phone, no Internet.

May the blessed "noise" of Christmas remind you of your need to be alone with God.

—————— ✳ ——————

Prayer: *Sweet hour of prayer, sweet hour of prayer, that calls me from a world of care*—Lord, I long for those times with you. Help me even in this busy season to plan to pray, in private and with my family. Amen.

Consider: Why is it hard for us to *get* alone with God? Why is it hard for us to *be* alone with God?

What are the most challenging obstacles for you to make or spend time alone with God? How can you intentionally remove these obstacles?

For Further Study and Reflection: What is the definition of an introvert? An extrovert? Which one are you? How does that impact your time alone with God?

Reflect: Ask yourself, *Do I need to spend more time alone with God? What would change about my life if I did?*

For Kids and Families: Ask, "Would you usually rather be alone or be with other people?" Give everyone a chance to share. Explain that even if we enjoy lots of time with other people, it's still important to spend time alone with God.

Talk about what time alone with God looks like (such as praying, listening, reading God's Word, memorizing scriptures, singing praises to God). If your children are old enough to be trusted to do so, give them five or ten minutes to spend alone with God. If the children are younger, model this time for them. Then come back together as a family and discuss how you spent your time alone with God and what your thoughts are about the experience.

———— ✳ ————

DECEMBER 15

Matthew 15 – Too Busy at Christmas?

Read Matthew 15:29–31

*The crowd wondered, when they saw the mute speaking,
the crippled healthy, the lame walking, and the blind seeing.
And they glorified the God of Israel. (Matthew 15:31)*

It was Christmas Eve. My kids were in town, the church office was closed, and the church staff members were celebrating with their families. I was at the church busy preparing for the Christmas Eve service. The phone rang: "I need gas in my car, diapers for the baby, and milk for my kids." I'm ashamed to confess that I wasn't thrilled. But I grabbed some diapers from the church nursery and met the caller at the gas station, where we bought gas and milk. Little did I know that that was the open door through which an entire family passed to meet Jesus!

Jesus always had something to do, but people kept coming to him, and they were desperate. Their friends and loved ones were sick and dying. They were handicapped and helpless. They needed a Healer, a Savior. These needy people were not the movers and shakers of society. They were not the wealthy and influential. They were poor and destitute, hopeless and insignificant.

When we say we want people to come to Jesus, who are we talking about? Do we want people whose lives are all put together, people who have great influence—in short, people who don't need much help but will instead help *us*? The crowds who came to Jesus beside the Sea of Galilee didn't feel that way. They brought the mute; Jesus loosened their tongues. They brought the crippled; Jesus made them well. They brought the lame; Jesus enabled them to walk. They brought the blind; Jesus opened their eyes.

Jesus came to seek and save the lost, to heal the sick, to set the captive free. Christmas is a good time to bring these people to Jesus. Will we do it, or are we too busy?

Prayer: Lord, forgive me for wanting to reach people who are like me to the exclusion of others. In this season help me to remember "the lame, the blind, the crippled, the mute, and many others." Amen.

Consider: Do you notice "the lame, the blind, the crippled, the mute" in your community? What are you doing to share the love of Christ with them?

At Christmas what can you do to develop attitudes and habits that will help you see them and reach them?

For Further Study and Reflection: Look up the demographics of your community. Are you in the majority or minority? Who are the people most unlike you in your community? In culture? In economics? In moral issues?

Reflect: Am I "filtering" my community before I bring them to Jesus?

For Kids and Families: Spend time looking through some family photos. Talk about how your family members are alike and different. Then use an Internet device to look up pictures of people from other ethnicities, countries, or cultures that are different from yours.

Discuss the fact that we often feel more comfortable around people we know well and are like us. Ask, "Why is it important to show love to people who are different from us? How did Jesus show us that this is important? How can we show love to someone who is different from us?"

———— ✳ ————

DECEMBER 16

Matthew 16 – Who Do You Say I Am?

Read Matthew 16:13–20

"But what about you?" he asked. "Who do you say I am?"
(Matthew 16:15 NIV)

Jesus asked his disciples, "Who do you say I am?" That's a good question at Christmas. Sadly, many people, if they think of Jesus at all, are confused about why we are talking about him: "What does Christmas have to do with Jesus? Christmas is about giving and getting, about family and fun, about parties and parades." Can you picture Jesus standing back, just scratching his head?

Would it be too much to expect at Christmas for us to ask ourselves, *Who do I say Jesus is?*

Who do you say Jesus is?

- Do you see Jesus as some sort of larger-than-life character, a legendary hero who is so perfect, so far above you that he is unconcerned with your life, too important to even notice you?

- Are you tempted to mold Jesus into your image—liking the same music, being of the same political party, getting annoyed over the same things? Is that who Jesus is—you with superpowers?

- Maybe you think of Jesus as a genie in a bottle. When you rub the bottle just right, he will grant you three wishes.

At first that's how Jesus's disciples saw him. But Jesus would have none of that. Even when they (correctly) responded that Jesus was the Son of God, their view of what that meant was woefully inadequate. When he told them what the Son of God would do—serve and sacrifice, submit and suffer—they said, "Never, Lord!"

This Christmas, who do you say that Jesus is? Is he the Lord of your life? Or are you still trying to call the shots? If we are really going to follow Jesus, we must deny ourselves, take up our crosses, and follow him in service and submission, suffering and sacrifice.

———— ✳ ————

Prayer: Lord, continue revealing yourself to me. I believe that my desire to follow your Word increases as I better understand just who you are. Help me to be a compassionate servant-leader just like King Jesus. I want to know you and I want my family to know you too. Amen.

Consider: Respond to this statement: "Christmas was traditionally a Christian festival celebrating the birth of Jesus, but in the early 20th century it also became a secular family holiday, observed by Christians and non-Christians alike" (Britannica.com).

Do you react to that negatively? Can it be seen in a positive way? How?

For Further Study and Reflection: Research the history of Christmas in the church vs. in the world. How and when did secular Christmas celebrations lose their connection to the Christian celebrations of Christmas? How has the church responded? Is it right to be defensive?

Reflect: How do my neighbors know what I think about Jesus? Does what I think make them want to know Jesus as I know Jesus?

For Kids and Families: Play a game of Christmas charades. Each family member will pick a Christmas character (such as a movie character, TV show character) and act out what that character would do or say. Family members try guessing the character.

After the game is over, talk with the children about the importance of knowing who Jesus is and that we should not try to make him into what we want him to be. What are some of Jesus's characteristics that we should emulate?

———— ✳ ————

DECEMBER 17

Matthew 17 – Terrified

Read Matthew 17:1–13

*When the disciples heard this, they fell on their faces
and were terrified.* (Matthew 17:6)

While on the mountaintop with Jesus, Peter, James, and John saw Jesus "transfigured before them, and his face shone like the sun, and his clothes became white as light" (Matthew 17:2). I would say that is a mountaintop experience, wouldn't you? But God wasn't done with them yet. He spoke to them—out loud! That was just too much for poor Peter, James, and John. They hit the ground, trembling with fear!

I believe that God wants to overwhelm us with his presence. But he knows that we are not ready. He knows that it would be like giving fire to a three-year-old. We would be consumed. His mercy prevents us from seeing his glory. Peter, James, and John were the only ones who were remotely ready on that day, and even they were terrified.

I once read that God has morphed in our minds from Holy Fire to Big Buddy. He is not a Holy Deity inspiring fear, but rather a Friendly Buddy inspiring fun. We traipse in and out of his sanctuary not expecting much to happen, not really preparing for an audience with this Terrifying Other.

This Christmas do you want the glory of God to shine around you? If so, get ready to be terrified—

> *And in the same region there were shepherds out in the field, keeping watch over their flock by night. And an angel of the Lord appeared to them, and the glory of the Lord shone around them, and they were filled with great fear.* (Luke 2:8–9)

———— ✳ ————

Prayer: Lord, forgive me for being so casual about your presence. Help me to approach you with reverence and in awe just as the shepherds did millennia ago. Amen.

Consider: What would have been your reaction if you were on the hillside with those shepherds on that first Christmas night?

How did the shepherds in the Bethlehem hills and the disciples on the Mount of Transfiguration react to the glory of God? How should we react to it? To its absence?

For Further Study and Reflection: Read Exodus 19; Exodus 34:1–9; and 1 Kings 18:20–39. What do they have in common? How are the circumstances and results different?

Reflect: When did you feel the presence and glory of God the strongest in your life? Do you long for another experience like it, or are you hoping it never happens again?

For Kids and Families: Ask, "When you're planning to go on a trip, what do you do to prepare?" Discuss this process, for example—creating a packing list, making reservations, preparing clothes, and so on. Remind the family that entering God's presence is something for which we should prepare, much like when we go on a trip.

Discuss:

• How do we prepare for entering God's presence? Allow everyone to share. Emphasize that we can prepare for God's presence by being open to him and what he wants to do in our lives.

• Remind everyone that we shouldn't be too casual about entering God's presence because he is worthy of our respect.

———— ✳ ————

DECEMBER 18

Matthew 18 – What Do You Think?

Read Matthew 18:1–14

*"What do you think? If a man has a hundred sheep,
and one of them has gone astray, does he not leave the
ninety-nine on the mountains and go in search of the
one that went astray?"* (Matthew 18:12)

Put yourself in this situation. You have a flock of one hundred sheep. Ninety-nine of them are safe in the fold with you. You are there to provide for them, to protect them, to guide them. But a helper comes to you and says, "That sheep that keeps wandering off . . . well, she's done it again!" What would you do? Would you leave the ninety-nine? Would you risk the many to save the one? Would you be able to explain it to the doubters and detractors? What do you think?

We know what Jesus, the Good Shepherd, thought. He left the comforts of heaven, he left the house of his Father, to "go in search of the one that went astray." I'm glad that he did, for I was that one. I was lost and had no way of finding my way back into the fold.

In this day of disinterest and even animosity toward Christ and the church, it is tempting to circle the wagons, to look inward, to count our losses, and to lick our wounds. But Jesus didn't adopt that attitude, did he? Christmas is a good time to be reminded that he doesn't want us to have that attitude either. We are to enlarge the kingdom, not to enclose it. We are to seek the lost sheep, not forget them.

What do you think?

———— ✳ ————

Prayer: You came to me, dear Jesus. Thank you so much for coming to me when I could not come to you.

Consider: Recall how you came to know Christ. Were you a child? A youth? An adult? Who were the "main players" in that process? Thank God for their influence, and if possible, reach out and thank them with a note, a call, or a visit.

Across the top of a blank sheet of paper write down these four headings: Family, Friends, Work/School, Neighbors. Now underneath these headings write the names of people who are "lost sheep." What can you do to lead them to the Good Shepherd?

For Further Study and Reflection: Research how many churches there are in the United States. What would happen if each church would reach ten "lost sheep" in the coming year?

Reflect: How can I be a part of my church reaching these "lost sheep"?

For Kids and Families: Get an empty jar or other container. Then give everyone in the family a small piece of paper. Ask, "Who is someone you could 'seek' after for Jesus?" Allow time for thinking and sharing. Have each member of the family write on the paper the name of someone he or she wants to influence for Christ. Put all the papers in the jar or container, and consider giving it a label, such as "Our Prayer Jar." Pray together for these people.

Place the jar or container in a visible location within your home to remind everyone to continue praying for these people and to actively reach out to them.

※

DECEMBER 19

Matthew 19 – A Perfect Christmas

Read Matthew 19:16–22

Jesus said to him, "If you would be perfect, go, sell what you possess and give to the poor, and you will have treasure in heaven; and come, follow me." (Matthew 19:21)

"That was a perfect Christmas!" I'm not sure we have ever been able to say that! We usually have something go wrong. One year the Christmas ham turned out to be spoiled. Another year everybody had to turn back due to the flu. Almost every year someone gets sick. (With nineteen people, when is someone *not* sick?). Perfection—even at Christmas—is elusive!

There once was a man seeking spiritual perfection. Jesus rocked his world when he said, *You can be perfect, but you have to give up everything to get it.*

Jesus dealt with the man's—

- **Will**: "If you would . . ." Do you really want this? If you don't desire this with all your heart and soul, then you won't get it.

- **Need**: "be perfect . . ." The Bible indicates that perfection is both obtainable and obligatory: "You therefore must be perfect, as your heavenly Father is perfect" (Matthew 5:48). The Greek word translated *perfect* means "brought to completion." We don't have God-like perfection, but we can be complete in the sight of God.

- **Obstacles**: "what you possess . . ." Jesus knows what is in a person (John 2:25), and he could read this man: *This guy likes money and the prestige it brings.*

- **Solution**: "go . . . sell . . . give . . ." Let go of all that stakes a greater claim on your heart than the claim of the kingdom. If it keeps you out of the kingdom, it's not worth having.

- **Reward**: "you will have treasure in heaven." When you've forsaken everything else, your treasure is in heaven.

- **Life**: "come, follow me . . ." Gaining the kingdom is less about making a decision for Christ and more about living a life with Christ.

Do you want a "perfect" Christmas and year to follow? It's possible to the fully surrendered heart!

———— ✳ ————

Prayer: Lord, I want my life to reflect you. Help me not to get caught up in the distraction of temporary gratification but instead focus on the eternal implications of my actions. Amen.

Consider: In what ways was the first Christmas in Bethlehem perfect? In what ways was it less than perfect?

Review the six requirements above: will, need, obstacles, solution, reward, and life. How did the Father and the Son meet those requirements to make Christmas perfect?

For Further Study and Reflection: Describe your idea of a perfect Christmas. What would you have to do to see it fulfilled?

Reflect: Extend these requirements for making your perfect Christmas to making a perfect life.

For Kids and Families: Remind the family that today's scripture deals with a young man who was too attached to his wealth. Discuss what barriers may be keeping your family from a more "perfect," or complete, relationship with Christ.

Decide as a family to do something that will move your relationship with Christ closer to perfection. Some examples: Use the money that would normally be spent on a meal at a restaurant to go shopping to purchase items for a local food pantry or homeless shelter; instead of watching a favorite television show, use this time to visit with a lonely elderly neighbor; give up electronic devices for a day and devote this time to family worship, prayer, and study of God's Word.

———— ✳ ————

DECEMBER 20

Matthew 20 – Begrudging Generosity

Read Matthew 20:1–16

"I choose to give to this last worker as I give to you.
Am I not allowed to do what I choose with what
belongs to me? Or do you begrudge my generosity?"
(Matthew 20:14–15)

"He's making a list. He's checking it twice. He's gonna find out who's naughty and nice. Santa Claus is comin' to town!" (Coots and Gillespie, 1934). Something about that ditty resonates with us—if we are some of the nice guys!

But Jesus, the real saint of the season, operates differently from Saint Nick.

In this parable of the vineyard, consider:

- The master of the house took the initiative (vv. 1, 3, 5, 6). He went out early to hire workers. After hiring those workers, he went out again to hire more. He went out again and again to hire still more. Aren't you glad that Jesus has taken the initiative? This is God's prevenient grace.

- The master chose (v. 14). Jesus said, "You did not choose me, but I chose you and appointed you that you should go and bear fruit" (John 15:16). We sometimes hear the slogan that says, "I choose Jesus," but the reality is that everyone who is saved was first chosen by Jesus! This is God's amazing grace!

- The master of the house gave (v. 14). The Bible says that "every good gift and every perfect gift is from above" (James 1:17). The laborers who were chosen were not earning their salvation. The ones who came at the eleventh hour received the same as those who responded at the beginning of the day. It was all a gift from the owner. If he had chosen workers at 11:59, who had not been able to get into the vineyard at all, they too would have been saved. This is God's unfailing grace.

Let Christmas remind you that God has indeed made a list. My name is on that list. Your name is on that list. Have you responded to God's grace?

———— ✳ ————

Prayer: Lord, thank you for your good gifts. You humbled yourself for me. You have given me the gift of salvation and paid the price for me. It is a gift I could never earn or deserve on my own. It is through you alone that I am saved. Thank you for your pursuit of my heart! Amen.

Consider: How did God take the initiative to save you, in general and specifically in your life? How have you responded to God's grace?

Is there someone you know who needs to hear the Christmas story as a story of grace? What will you do to share that story?

For Further Study and Reflection: Listen to or read the lyrics of "Santa Claus Is Comin' to Town." How do these words reflect or contradict the grace of God?

Reflect: What in my life would indicate that I view God as Santa Claus—or that I view him as the master of the vineyard as seen in this parable? How should I respond to this knowledge?

For Kids and Families: As a family, search the Internet for ways the figure of Saint Nicholas/Santa is portrayed in cultures different from your own. Allow each member of the family to share what he or she learned that was interesting or surprising.

Make a list of the ways God is like Santa. Make a list of the ways God is different from Santa. Emphasize that God in his great grace has chosen us and given generously to us.

————— ✳ —————

DECEMBER 21

Matthew 21 – What Does He Say?

Read Matthew 21:28–32

"Which of the two did the will of his father?"
(Matthew 21:31)

Matt, our mission team leader, made sure we had our passports ready, and he gave us specific instructions on how to navigate through customs as we headed back into the United States. Those instructions did not include saying clever things. As a matter of fact, he told us not to say anything but answer the questions! "These guys are serious," he said. As I passed through customs, I quickly discovered that they were indeed serious! And I can assure you that I could not have talked my way through customs. But I didn't need to. I had my passport ready, and the agent said, "Welcome home."

It's not what we say to God that's important. Rather, it's what he says to us: "Well done, good and faithful servant. . . . Enter into the joy of your master" (Matthew 25:21). In Matthew 21 Jesus tells the story about a man who sent his two sons to work in his vineyard. One of them said he would—and didn't. The other said he wouldn't—and did. "Which of the two did the will of his father?" (v. 31).

The religious folks of Jesus's day thought that by saying the right things about God they would be okay. But Jesus blasted their self-righteousness: "The tax collectors and the prostitutes go into the kingdom of God before you" (v. 31). Jesus showed them that it's not the respectable or those who say the right things who are acceptable. It's the broken who humble themselves in repentance, faith, and obedience who are accepted.

Christmas is a reminder that Jesus Christ—who came in humility and obedience—has shown us the way to the Father. He has given us the passport! Do you have your passport ready?

Prayer: Lord, sometimes I overlook the instructions because I assume I know what to do. Your Word is meant to be read, known, and followed. Help me to do just that. Amen.

Consider: Is it easier to get out of Mexico or to get into the United States? I have been told that once people step onto the north side of the Rio Grande, they are in the United States. Depending on the time of year, that is relatively easy. But then they face the border wall. That is much harder. You may say, "They are part and parcel of the same thing," and I would agree. But you can't make it into the US without leaving Mexico. The same is true of the kingdom of heaven. You cannot enter it without leaving your life of sin. Have you left sin and entered the kingdom of God? Have you done the will of the Father or just said you would?

For Further Study and Reflection: Research the requirements to enter the United States. What happens to people who show up at customs without their passports?

Reflect: First Thessalonians 4:3 says, "This is the will of God, your sanctification." Am I living in the will of God?

For Kids and Families: Ask the family, "If there was a ticket to get into heaven, what would it look like?" Give everyone a piece of paper and five minutes to design a ticket to heaven. Allow each one to share his or her ideas about what this could look like.

Remind the family that our "ticket" to heaven is Jesus. He paid our "admission" and bought our "tickets." All we have to do it accept this and live for him!

———— ✳ ————

✝

DECEMBER 22

Matthew 22 – Welcome and Wanted

Read Matthew 22:1–14

"'Go therefore to the main roads and invite to the wedding feast as many as you find.' And those servants went out into the roads and gathered all whom they found, both bad and good. So the wedding hall was filled with guests." (Matthew 22:9–10)

The king wanted as many as possible to attend the wedding of his son. So he sent his faithful servants out to call in those who had been invited. Those servants, however, were ignored and abused. Some were even killed. Eager for people to celebrate with him and his son, the king sent servants out again to "invite to the wedding feast as many as you find" (v. 9). So the servants did just that, reaching out to the good and the bad—and the banquet was a huge success!

It is obvious who the characters are in this parable. The king is God the Father. He desires that all would come to the wedding banquet. So he has sent his faithful servants with the good news that everyone is welcome and wanted—*Please come now!* Those who are being invited represent all the people of the world, both good and bad. God is no respecter of persons but is willing that all should come to repentance and come into the kingdom. There is no one outside the loving reach and purpose of God. Some will refuse and abuse, but all are welcome and wanted.

But what about the son in this story? In Matthew 21 Jesus explained that he too had been sent by his Father. But those to whom he was sent rejected him: "This is the heir. Come, let us kill him and have his inheritance" (v. 38). Christmas reveals to us the great love of the Father who sent his Son to do battle for our souls. And because of that, we have been invited to the eternal banquet.

This Christmas as you consider the Babe in Bethlehem, remember that you are welcome and wanted!

Prayer: Father, forgive me for thinking that some are just not good enough to be invited. I know that you invite everyone, even me! Use me to gather "both bad and good" so that heaven may be filled with guests. Amen.

Consider: Have you ever been the guest in another family's Christmas or other special celebration? How did you feel? What did your hosts do to make you feel welcome and wanted?

Have you ever invited an outsider into one of your family celebrations? How did your other family members feel about it? How did you help everybody enjoy the time together?

For Further Study and Reflection: What makes people feel unwanted by God? Unwanted at church? (You can find lots of lists online about why people don't go to church. You have to dig a little deeper to find why they feel unwanted, but it is worth the "dig.")

Reflect: Does the above make me feel defensive? Are some of the reasons hypocritical in themselves? What can I do to make people feel welcome and wanted? Are there areas I will not compromise on to make people feel welcome? What are they?

For Kids and Families: Offer a choice of snacks to the family, stipulating that each person can choose only one item. For example, allow each person to choose a cookie or some popcorn. Remind everyone that sometimes we make choices when it comes to including people. Today's scripture points out that everyone is chosen by God.

Have everyone think of a person he or she knows who may often feel unchosen or frequently left out by others. Discuss ways of making these people feel more included and loved.

————— ✳ —————

✝

DECEMBER 23

Matthew 23 – Greatest of All Time

Read Matthew 23:1–15

"The greatest among you shall be your servant.
Whoever exalts himself will be humbled, and
whoever humbles himself will be exalted."
(Matthew 23:11–12)

Lana and I recently purchased an "early Christmas gift" for ourselves—a car. (We do that a lot for gift-giving—give each other big-ticket items that we need to buy anyway. It makes it a little more fun, and we can talk about the great Christmas gifts we got!) After we closed the deal on the car, the salesperson, Janetta, asked me to fill out a Google review. I promptly told her that as a salesperson she was the GOAT, thinking that she knew what I meant. Her demeanor told me that she did not understand, and I quickly explained that GOAT means "greatest of all time." That satisfied her!

The Pharisees of Jesus's day were convinced that they were GOATs. They sought out special privileges, perks, and praise for themselves. Jesus quickly corrected them and told them true GOATs humble themselves and serve others.

Jesus, who truly was the greatest of all time, didn't consider it beneath his dignity to visit the sick, the dying, the poor, the possessed, and yes, the sinful. He wasn't looking to gain notoriety. He sought to change lives. And that's what he wants us to do too. If we want to be GOATs, our focus must be on serving others. No one else may ever know it. That's okay. Jesus sees every act of kindness, every deed of service, every offer of assistance.

We are enjoying our new car, but it's not the GOAT. When it comes to the greatest of all Christmas gifts, we know who the GOAT is, don't we? It is Jesus! Have you received *that* Christmas gift?

———— ✳ ————

Prayer: Lord, sometimes serving others doesn't come naturally to me. You call me to value others above myself. Help me to love and serve the people around me the way that you would—filled with love, free from grumbling, and with no thought of public praise. Amen.

Consider: How did Jesus, as the greatest of all time, display servanthood? Read Philippians 2:1–11. How can you have the same mind that was in Christ?

What are some practical ways today that you can serve others? Does the Christmas season offer you unique opportunities to serve others? How will you respond to them specifically?

For Further Study and Reflection: Research "servant leadership" online or reflect on how you think it looks. Does it "go against the grain" in your mind? How did Jesus display servant leadership? How can you display servant leadership?

Reflect: Kathleen Patterson in her 2003 dissertation identified these seven facets of servant leadership: love, humility, altruism, vision, trust, empowerment, and service. Which areas are you strong in? Weak? What can you do to improve?

For Kids and Families: Remind the family that in today's scripture we learn that to be the greatest, we must serve others.

Discuss ways to do this. How can we serve others in our homes? In our schools? In our churches?

—————— ✳ ——————

DECEMBER 24

Matthew 24 – Are You Ready?

Read Matthew 24:36–44

"Therefore you also must be ready, for the Son of Man is coming at an hour you do not expect." (Matthew 24:44)

Christmas is almost here. Are you ready?

- Mary and Joseph were. They had believed God and had kept the faith throughout an arduous journey.

- The shepherds were not. They were taken totally off guard by the angelic announcement.

- The wise men were. They traveled for months to welcome Jesus.

- Herod was not. He thought *he* was the king of the Jews!

Being ready for Jesus's first coming was important, but being ready for his *second* coming is even more so!

In Matthew 24 Jesus answers the big question "How can I be ready?" We must keep watch:

- We must keep watch over the developing situations of the world. The "increase of wickedness," the "love of many growing cold," "false prophets"—these remind us that Jesus's coming is near.

- We must keep watch, therefore, over our souls. In these "last days," spiritual disciplines have fallen on hard times. We are careless in the care of our souls. However, in this day of increasing evil we must give attention not just to the state but also to the state *of our souls.*

- Finally, we must keep watch over the souls of our family, fellow Christians, friends, and neighbors. What are we doing to "give them their food at the proper time" (v. 45)? What are we doing to ensure that the lost hear the message, to encourage struggling Christians, or to teach the next generation the truth?

The One whose first coming is celebrated tomorrow is coming again. Are you ready?

———— ✳ ————

Prayer: Thank you, Lord Jesus, that you came to earth 2,000 years ago. And thank you for the promise of your return. And though I may not have all the symbolism and timing figured out, I can be ready by trusting in you, and you alone, for salvation. Help me to keep watch! Amen.

Consider: How have you prepared for Christmas? Are you ready? If not, what yet do you need to do?

In this journey through Advent, you have been preparing spiritually for the coming of Christ. Have you accomplished that? If not, what is there yet to do?

For Further Study and Reflection: Prayerfully go back through each day's "Consider" and "For Further Study and Reflection." Is there something you need to do in response?

Reflect: How am I to keep watch over the situations of the world? The state of my soul? The souls of my family?

For Kids and Families: As a family, make some sort of last-minute preparation for tomorrow's Christmas celebrations. For example, set out cookies and milk for Santa, wrap a present that is still unwrapped, or work together to prepare food for tomorrow.

Remind the family that this task is a fun part of preparing for Christmas. However, this is not the most important task we need to do. The most important is to be ready for Christ's coming at Christmastime and when he returns for his second coming. Pray together as a family, asking God to help us be constantly prepared for his arrival.

DECEMBER 25

Merry Christmas!

Read Luke 2:1–20

1 In those days a decree went out from Caesar Augustus that all the world should be registered. ² This was the first registration when Quirinius was governor of Syria. ³ And all went to be registered, each to his own town. ⁴ And Joseph also went up from Galilee, from the town of Nazareth, to Judea, to the city of David, which is called Bethlehem, because he was of the house and lineage of David, ⁵ to be registered with Mary, his betrothed, who was with child. ⁶ And while they were there, the time came for her to give birth. ⁷ And she gave birth to her firstborn son and wrapped him in swaddling cloths and laid him in a manger, because there was no place for them in the inn.

⁸ And in the same region there were shepherds out in the field, keeping watch over their flock by night. ⁹ And an

angel of the Lord appeared to them, and the glory of the Lord shone around them, and they were filled with great fear. [10] And the angel said to them, "Fear not, for behold, I bring you good news of great joy that will be for all the people.[11] For unto you is born this day in the city of David a Savior, who is Christ the Lord. [12] And this will be a sign for you: you will find a baby wrapped in swaddling cloths and lying in a manger."

[13] And suddenly there was with the angel a multitude of the heavenly host praising God and saying, [14] "Glory to God in the highest, and on earth peace among those with whom he is pleased!"

[15] When the angels went away from them into heaven, the shepherds said to one another, "Let us go over to Bethlehem and see this thing that has happened, which the Lord has made known to us." [16] And they went with haste and found Mary and Joseph, and the baby lying in a manger. [17] And when they saw it, they made known the saying that had been told them concerning this child.

[18] And all who heard it wondered at what the shepherds told them. [19] But Mary treasured up all these things, pondering them in her heart. [20] And the shepherds returned, glorifying and praising God for all they had heard and seen, as it had been told them.

Prayer:

> Jesus, we recall on Christmas morn,
>
> Just how you came to be born.
>
> In stable low, in cattle stall,
>
> You humbly came to save us all.
>
> May we, this day, each do our part,
>
> Asking you to come into our heart.
>
> Amen.

For Everyone:

After reading the Christmas story together, talk about the importance of this story. Discuss ways you can keep the spirit of Christmas alive beyond this day.

DECEMBER 26

Matthew 25 – Keep Watch

Matthew 25:1–13

*"Watch therefore, for you know neither the
day nor the hour."* (Matthew 25:13)

I know that in six days the new year will begin. I know
the exact time it will be here. As I write this devotional, however, I find myself keeping watch out the front
window for "Mr. Appliance." I know he's coming, but
I don't know the exact time of his arrival. So I am watching.

We know that Jesus is coming too. Sorry to cause you anxiety, but it's more a "Mr. Appliance" thing than a new year
thing. So we *keep watch*.

What does it mean to *keep watch*? We see it vividly portrayed in the next chapter regarding the garden of Gethsemane:

- It means to pray. In Gethsemane Jesus told his disciples to "watch and pray." The same applies for our watching today. As we wait for the return of Jesus, it is imperative that we pray. We will face tribulations as the Lord's return nears, and our strength in trial depends upon our intimacy with the Father.

- It means to stay awake. The problem with the prayerless disciples was not unwillingness but sleepiness: "The spirit indeed is willing, but the flesh is weak" (Matthew 26:41). How true that is! If we are not careful, our culture will numb us into a state of lethargy and apathy.

- It means to focus on spiritual things. When Jesus left to pray, the disciples lost their focus. God is always speaking, but we must be listening.

- It means to guard those entrusted to us. Jesus knew that danger was coming. He wanted his most trusted friends to prepare both him and the others for the arrival of Judas and the guards. We not only must keep watch for ourselves, but we also must keep watch for those we love.

Keep watch!

Prayer: Lord, I thank you that you have warned us to keep watch. In this new year help me to live ready for your return— constant in prayer, wide awake, spiritually engaged, and watching over others. Amen.

———— ✳ ————

✝

DECEMBER 27

Matthew 25 – Doing Well

Matthew 25:14–30

"'Well done, good and faithful servant. You have been faithful over a little; I will set you over much. Enter into the joy of your master.'" (Matthew 25:21)

The end of the year is a good time to stop and see how you are doing, to make sure you are doing well.

Before we retired from the pastorate, Lana and I met with our financial advisor several times to see how we were doing financially. Can you imagine our reaction if he had told us, "I'm sorry, but I didn't know what to do with your money, so I just buried it in my backyard. After all, I didn't want to lose any of it. So here it is! You can thank me later!" To say the least, we would not have been happy!

Just as Lana and I entrusted our funds to a financial advisor, Jesus has entrusted us with kingdom assets. Would he be pleased if we neglected their proper use, or, even worse, if we used them for our own selfish ends?

How are you using the talents he has given you? Are you investing them in kingdom priorities and values—winning the lost, showing forth God's glory, spreading the kingdom's love, and caring for the needy? In short, are you doing well?

"Well done!" If we want to hear those words, then we must *do* well! He has given all of us specific responsibilities in accordance with our abilities. None of us is exempt from these assignments. He didn't save us so that we could sit and wait. He saved us to do good things and to do them well.

I hope you are doing well.

Prayer: I recognize, O Lord God, that you have given me talents and resources and opportunities to use for you. Today and all through the coming year, help me to be faithful over this "little," that I will one day hear those blessed words, "Well done!" Amen.

---- ✳ ----

DECEMBER 28

Matthew 26 – A Beautiful Thing

Matthew 26:6–13

"She has done a beautiful thing to me." (Matthew 26:10)

I t is the nature of love to give, and sometimes love just needs to be extravagant. That is what happened with the woman in Matthew 26, the woman who anointed Jesus with "very expensive ointment" (v. 7). Some scholars believe the alabaster flask of oil cost a year's wages. It quite possibly could have represented her life's savings.

When we are in love with Christ, there are times when our "reason" is thrown out the window. It was not reasonable for this woman to make such a statement of love. Why, if nothing else, the ointment could have been sold and the money given to the poor! Your love for Christ, including sacrificial giving and service, passionate worship and prayer, will be misunderstood and denigrated by those who know nothing of what Christ's sacrifice has done for you: the life he gives you, the peace that surrounds you, the joy that strengthens you, the love that fills you.

And don't forget—this beautiful deed left a lasting fragrance. Not only was the house filled with the aroma of this sacrifice, but history itself has preserved the pleasing scent of love. Love has a ripple effect that expands and expands.

Another thing this story teaches me is that there are certain things that must be done when the opportunity avails itself. As in Robert Frost's "The Road Not Taken," we come to diverging paths in the woods. What we choose will determine our course of life. The woman who anointed Jesus "took the one less traveled by, and that has made all the difference." What choices are you pondering?

Do beautiful things for Jesus today and all year long!

Prayer: Jesus, thank you for your extravagant love for me. I want to be extravagant in my response. I give you my heart and life today. In every day of the coming year, may I do something beautiful for you. Amen.

———— ✶ ————

DECEMBER 29

Matthew 26 – Willing Spirit; Weak Flesh

Read Matthew 26:35–41

"Watch and pray that you may not enter into temptation. The spirit indeed is willing, but the flesh is weak." (Matthew 26:41)

Have you ever bragged like Peter when he said, "Even if I must die with you, I will not deny you!" (v. 35)? Did your subsequent actions support your claim, whatever it was?

We can learn from Peter's weakness:

• Peter made his claim in front of the other disciples, and then they "said the same" (v. 35). There is something about being with a crowd of enthusiastic and bombastic people that causes us to boast. We want to appear to be strong, superior, invincible. This year be very careful about what you claim before others. Both you and they may have to eat a little crow!

- When Peter had the opportunity to pray for Jesus, he slept! Despite repeated warnings, Peter just couldn't make himself pray. The time we need prayer the most is when we find it the hardest to pray. This year try to get better at pushing through the hindrances to prayer.

- Peter was indeed a courageous man, but the flesh that was weak in spiritual warfare proved to be weak in physical crisis. The flesh will revolt against us in times of crisis. This year determine to pray, to garner strength and courage for the battle!

- "When you fail to plan, you plan to fail." Even truer: "When you fail to pray, you plan to fail." Watchful prayer is the most effective barrier to spiritual failure, to emotional fatigue, to bad attitudes, and to poor decisions. One hour spent in prayer, in the Scriptures, and in spiritual reflection prepares you for twenty-three hours on the go! This year make a specific prayer plan.

Prayer: Lord, I don't want to be a person of empty claims and broken promises. Help me to garner strength from you. In the coming year help me to develop a habit and pattern of daily prayer. Amen.

———— ✳ ————

DECEMBER 30

Matthew 27 – What Do I Want?

Matthew 27:50–61

He went to Pilate and asked for the body of Jesus.
(Matthew 27:58)

When I retired, I "packed up my office" over the course of several weeks, moving library and files to my home office. I'm glad I gave myself adequate time, for I quickly discovered that I had accumulated lots of "stuff" in thirty-one years of ministry! I found that I need to be selective about what to keep. There's just not space for everything. "Do I really want that?"

Times come when we have to ask ourselves, "Do I want that? Do I need it?" Those questions are hard but necessary.

In Matthew 27 Joseph of Arimathea wanted something—the body of Jesus. So he went to Pilate and asked for it. I'm sure Pilate found that an unusual request. Often the bodies of condemned criminals were simply discarded in a pit near the place of execution. When they were taken, though, it was by grieving family members. But here was a respectable and well-to-do Jewish citizen, unrelated to Jesus, asking for the body. Why would he want the body of the Lord? *Oh, well,* Pilate thought. *I guess he can have it.*

How about you? Do you want the body of Jesus? Will you identify with the stigma of the cross, that sign of weakness and symbol of death? It is easy to want the *resurrected* body of Jesus. But the body of *death*? The apostle Paul said that we are "always carrying in the body the death of Jesus, so that the life of Jesus may also be manifested in our bodies" (2 Corinthians 4:10).

One final question. What problem, bitterness, failure, or anger are you taking into the new year? Do you really want that? Should you not rather be taking the body of Jesus?

Prayer: Jesus, how incredible that you, the Son of God, would die for me. I gladly identify with you in your death so that your life may be manifested in me today and every day in the new year. Amen.

———— ✳ ————

DECEMBER 31

Matthew 28 – Come and See. Go and Tell.

Read Matthew 28:1–10

"Do not be afraid, for I know that you seek Jesus who was crucified. He is not here, for he has risen, as he said. Come, see the place where he lay. Then go quickly and tell his disciples that he has risen from the dead." (Matthew 28:5–7)

You seek Jesus. He is not here, for he has risen.

Death was not the final word in Jesus's life, and it is not the final word in this year either. At times we are tempted to despair, to give up. But no place is so dark that the light of Jesus cannot penetrate it. If death was not a barrier to God's power and grace, then nothing is!

As we conclude this year and begin a new one, consider the words of that angel to those women at the empty tomb of Jesus:

- *Come . . . see.* Sometimes we must look our problems square in the eye. To be delivered from our "demons," we must confront them, see them—but do so in light of the resurrection! The tomb is empty! Death has lost its sting!

- *Go . . . tell.* One of the best ways to "cement" our faith is to testify to what we have discovered and experienced. Jesus is alive! Jesus has delivered me! How many do you know who need to hear this message of hope? Tell them!

So "Do not be afraid!" He has already gone before you into the new year!

A blessing from the author
"The Lord bless you and keep you;
the Lord make his face to shine upon you
and be gracious to you;
the Lord lift up his countenance upon you
and give you peace."
Amen.
(Numbers 6:24–26)

OTHER BOOKS BY SCOTT WADE

CHRISTMAS WITH LUKE (English)
LA NAVIDAD CON LUCAS (Spanish)
NATAL COM LUCAS (Portuguese)

THE CLIMB
A five-year devotional guide through the Bible
Book 1: ***START HERE***
Book 2: ***STAY FOCUSED***
Book 3: ***STICK WITH IT***
Book 4: ***STRETCH YOURSELF***
Book 5: ***STAND TALL***

. . . .

How to order:
Visit Momentum Ministries website at
www.momentumministries.org
to order copies of this and other books to help you attain,
maintain, and regain spiritual momentum.

ABOUT THE AUTHORS

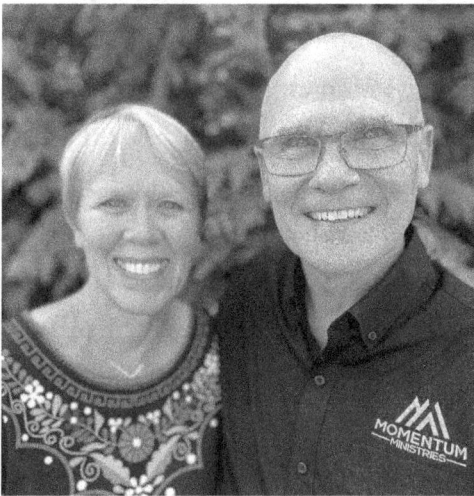

Evangelist SCOTT WADE is the founder and president of Momentum Ministries, seeking to help people attain, maintain, and regain spiritual momentum. In addition to preaching, Scott has authored seven books and various other materials. He publishes a weekly podcast, distributes a weekly video, and leads mission teams in sharing the gospel of Jesus Christ.

Prior to leading Momentum Ministries, Scott served as a pastor for over thirty years. Whether in North Carolina, Illinois, Ohio, or South Carolina, he faced the annual challenge of engaging congregations of various sizes and backgrounds in the message of Christmas.

Scott and his wife, Lana, have grounded this season on the Word of God. In Christmas musicals, holiday sermons, and family Advent observations, the Bible was their guide. Out of this conviction arose the idea to provide individuals, families, and churches with a biblically based Advent journey. The first volume, *Christmas with Luke*, published in 2019, was received enthusiastically by congregations and individuals, and many encouraged Scott to write a complementary volume. Once again Scott has partnered with Matt and Fay Wagner to provide a meaningful Advent experience for children as well as for teens and adults: *Christmas with Matthew*.

Scott continues writing and preaching the Word. From their base in South Carolina, the Wades conduct revivals (providing both message and music if needed) wherever God leads and churches call.

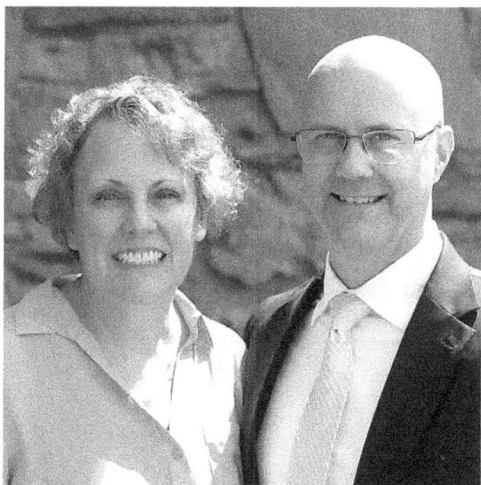

MATT and FAY WAGNER are lifelong educators, having served in public schools in North Carolina and Ohio both in the classroom and administration. Alongside their educational careers, the Wagners served faithfully in their local churches and have led many mission trips, both foreign and domestic. They are now following the call of God to serve in longer-term mission assignments. And when they are available, they serve on the Momentum Ministries evangelistic team with the Wades.

✻

www.ingramcontent.com/pod-product-compliance
Lightning Source LLC
Chambersburg PA
CBHW061733020426
42331CB00006B/1229